To Jacque
My love

Love Mom

Lessons My *Momma* Taught Me

Absolutely Nothing Will Ever Take the Place of the Love and Lessons Shared between a Mother and Her Children

CARLA JACKSON

Scriptures taken from the Holy Bible, New International Version®, NIV®. Copyright © 1973, 1978, 1984, 2011 by Biblica, Inc.™ Used by permission of Zondervan. All rights reserved worldwide. www.zondervan.com The "NIV" and "New International Version" are trademarks registered in the United States Patent and Trademark Office by Biblica, Inc.™ All rights reserved.

This book is a work of non-fiction. Unless otherwise noted, the author and the publisher make no explicit guarantees as to the accuracy of the information contained in this book and in some cases, names of people and places have been altered to protect their privacy.

ISBN: 978-1-4834-5981-3 (sc)
ISBN: 978-1-4834-5982-0 (e)

Library of Congress Control Number: 2016916747

Because of the dynamic nature of the Internet, any web addresses or links contained in this book may have changed since publication and may no longer be valid. The views expressed in this work are solely those of the author and do not necessarily reflect the views of the publisher, and the publisher hereby disclaims any responsibility for them.

Any people depicted in stock imagery provided by Thinkstock are models, and such images are being used for illustrative purposes only. Certain stock imagery © Thinkstock.

Lulu Publishing Services rev. date: 3/27/2017

Dedications

To my beautiful mother, Ora, your unwavering love will forever be a part of my heart. There will never be anyone who could ever take your place. I am the woman I am today because of who you were to me. Thank you for instilling morals and values that shaped my being. Thank you for imparting the importance of knowing Christ by being a living and loving example. You were the best mother ever. I know that you are now sleeping with angels. I have the faith that we will be together again someday. Sweet rest, Mother. Sweet rest...

To my wonderful husband, Robert, thank you for your unwavering love and support. You entered my life when I needed you most. Your belief in me continues to give me the courage that I need to help me pursue the unthinkable. You are my soul mate, my lover, and my best friend. I love you, Honeylumps.

To my children, Jacques, Joy, Victoria, and Robert II, thank you for your love. I am who I am because of the love we share. Being a mother completes me.

To my precious grandson, Braylon, there's nothing more rewarding than hearing you call me "Nana" when you need me the most. You are a precious blessing from heaven above.

To my beautiful sisters, Sheila, Sheryl, Charlotte, Mona, Bobbie, and Yolande...all of you are the wind beneath my wings. We are definitely "Ora's Girls." I love each of you very much, and your love and support means the world to me.

To my loving dads, Douglas and Curtis, your strength and timeless love will forever be in my heart.

To my selfless and beautiful cousin Cassondra aka *Michelle*, thank you for taking the time to bless me with your master skill of editing during your time of loss. Love you.

-Momma-
"A mother's love knows no bounds and will always
be there when you need it the most." Carla J

Contents

(L-R) Ora's Girls-- Bobbie, Sheryl, Sheila,
Carla, Mona, Charlotte, and Yolande
"Sisters are beautiful pillars of strength who hold each
other up and make life worth living." Carla J

$\mathcal{I}$ntroduction

My mother was a beautiful, feisty woman. She and her brother and four sisters grew up poor. She was the oldest of the girls and always felt as if she had to make the most sacrifices, especially when the family's finances were scarce. Her parents divorced when she was in her mid-teens, so she left school in the middle of her eighth grade year to help support her family, toiling in the cotton fields of west Texas for long, hot hours every weekday.

My mother frequently shared stories with my sisters and me of picking cotton alongside her mama. Although those were some very difficult times, my mother said she never complained because she loved her mama dearly and felt one of her major goals in life was to keep her mama happy.

While growing up, my six siblings and I often gathered around my mother's feet as she sat in her favorite chair. We listened attentively as she told us stories from her past. Because she was poor, many of the stories she shared were difficult to hear, but we loved to hear her speak. My mother also had an angelic singing voice. In the mornings, while preparing breakfast for my sisters and me, she often sang spiritual hymns. Sometimes she cried while she sang. When we asked her why was she crying, she'd say, "I'm just thinking about the goodness of God. He's been just that good."

My mother taught all of her girls how to survive on very little or next to nothing. She said there were certain ingredients that every household with children should always have on hand to ensure that no one would ever go hungry: flour, sugar, eggs, milk, baking powder, rice, and beans. "If you keep these things in your cupboard or refrigerator, you can make just about anything that's going to taste good, and it will fill you up until 'better' comes along," she'd say. She was right, too. To this day, those items are staple ingredients in my home that I never run out of; not just because I use them regularly, but because of what my mother taught me.

While growing up, I witnessed my mother work many jobs. She worked long hours and was exhausted when she got home. She drove a school bus for fifteen years. She was a woman who did whatever she had to do to raise God-fearing and loving girls who would grow up possessing a lifelong passion for family and faith.

My dad suffered from alcoholism and mental illness while my sisters and I were young. He would often get paid on Fridays and wouldn't make it home until either late Sunday evening or early Monday morning. Oftentimes, I could hear my mother arguing with my dad because not only would he come home with a huge hangover, he would also have spent all of his earnings from the previous week. My dad never argued with her. I could tell he felt badly about what he'd done, but his addiction to alcohol and his suffering with mental illness weighed heavier on him than his concern for providing for his family. Finally, one day my mother said she had had enough of my dad's lack of support and told him to pack his things and get out. Although Dad wasn't a great provider, he was still my dad. Seeing him put all his belongings in a white pillowcase and walk out the front door was probably one of the saddest things a five-year-old should have to witness.

After my dad left, my mother gathered my sisters and me in the living room and told us that Dad was no longer going to live with us and that she was going to have to get a job—actually several jobs to make ends meet. She also told two of my older sisters that they were going to have to pick up the slack and take care of my younger siblings and me. My mother was a proud woman. She never wanted government assistance, but after my father left, she didn't have much of a choice. I vividly remember trying to get used to eating cooked powdered eggs and drinking mixed powdered milk. Those were two of the most disgusting things I had ever put in my mouth. I don't quite remember how it made it into our home, but sometime around the first of each month, we received a huge block of cheese, aptly called "government cheese." It came in a big, brown rectangular cardboard box. It was actually quite good. My sisters and I liked to cut off big chunks and place them on slices of bread, then put them in the bottom of our gas stove and make grilled cheese sandwiches. Those were the absolute best grilled cheese sandwiches ever!

We had to get on food stamps, too. My mother occasionally sent us to the neighborhood store to pick up different things for the house. Because you could not buy toiletries or cleaning supplies with food stamps, my mother worked out an agreement with the Asian owner of the neighborhood grocery store to purchase those items with the stamps in a little back room of the store. It never really felt quite right, but my sisters and I knew better than to ask questions. We could tell my mother was not comfortable with that agreement. But I now know that my mother was doing the very best she knew how to do when it came to providing for her children. After all, for a woman with only an eighth grade education to raise seven children by herself was not an easy task. Not by a long shot!

As a young child, my family and I lived in the Cuney Homes project apartments located in the Third Ward area of Houston, Texas. Most or all of the occupants' rent was paid with government subsidies. Yes, we were poor, and yes, we lived in the projects, but honestly, some of my most treasured memories of growing up were lived out in the projects. My family and our friends knew we were poor, but we didn't allow our economic circumstances to prevent us from enjoying our youth. It's amazing what children can come up with to entertain themselves when their options are few.

Although my mother usually worked multiple jobs at the same time, she rarely had any money left over for things other than the bare necessities. Along with providing the necessities, my mother also made sure we were respectful toward others, always safe, and greatly loved. She often said, "Girls, we may not have much, but we have Jesus and each other and that's more than enough."

I vividly remember not being able to afford popsicles from the ice cream truck that came around in the evenings, especially in the summertime. Summers in Houston were extremely hot and ice cream and popsicles made the heat just a little bit more bearable. All that red brick the apartments in the projects were made out of didn't help things, either.

Once, on a sweltering afternoon after watching my friends purchase ice cream from the ice cream truck, my mother called for my siblings and me to come inside. When we got in the apartment, much to our surprise, our mother had homemade popsicles waiting for us. Although the popsicles did not look anything like the popsicles sold by the ice cream man, they were good! We immediately ran back outside with our newly-made cold creations. Our friends were so impressed with our homemade treats they started placing orders with my mom. My mother affectionately became known as the "Cool Cup Lady." No pun intended, but my sisters and I thought that was the "coolest" thing ever because we finally had something that our peers wanted. That was really a great feeling.

I also vividly remember frequently wishing and hoping that the day would come when my mother would have just enough money to purchase something that I'd longed for and dreamed about practically every night—a red "Big Chief" tablet notebook that had at least fifty sheets instead of the normal amount of just twenty-five sheets. Most of my classmates' parents could afford to buy them the Big Chief tablet with fifty sheets. My heart sank when my teacher had us write. Most of my classmates would pull out their big red Big Chief tablet with fifty sheets and I had to pull out mine that only contained half the sheets, and to add insult to injury, I usually ran out of paper and had to frequently borrow sheets of paper from my peers. Oh my God, that was so embarrassing! I dreamed day and night for a Big Chief tablet that had more than twenty-five sheets. Needless to say, I never got one. Raising six children at the time as a single parent for my mother was not easy and getting a big red Big Chief tablet with more than twenty-five sheets simply wasn't a priority.

My mom was an old-fashioned mother, too. She did not allow any of her girls to be disrespectful or to be disrespected. She took us to church every Sunday. By her example, she taught us to be upstanding and God-fearing girls. Every morning and every night my mother would get on her knees and pray to God. Early one morning after hearing her pray, I asked her why she'd continue praying every morning and every night when it appeared to me that things weren't changing. We were still quite poor—and I never got that Big Chief tablet, either. I thought to myself that God wasn't listening to me or my mother's prayers. Her quick response remains with me to this very day, "Girl, let me tell you something. You don't praise God for what He does—you praise Him for who He is! Now get out of my room!" Hearing her say that confirmed for me that she was communicating with a worthy God. It also helped me to take the focus off of me and to stop feeling sorry for myself, especially over a little notebook. That response really gave me hope.

My mother was a wise woman. Although she had a limited education, she spoke words of deep wisdom every single day of my life. That's a major reason why my sisters and I could sit at her feet for hours, listening to her impart sage words that would remain with us for a lifetime. She would often say that she was just passing on the wisdom that her mama had lovingly passed on to her. She would also say, "What good is wisdom if you're going to be stingy with it? I'm not a stingy person and my girls won't be stingy, either."

The stories that my mother frequently shared with us and the lessons she taught by example inevitably made me want to be a better person. The stories she told us also helped us to better understand her journey which framed the decisions she made and the things she said—and allowed me to fully understand the infinity of her never-wavering love for all of her girls.

One particular story my mother told still resonates deeply with me even to this very day. It happened when my siblings and I were really young. My mother was pregnant with my second-youngest sibling, Bobbie Jean. She said she had gone outside to hang clothes on the clothing line in our backyard while wearing shoes that had a small heel—the only pair of shoes she owned at the time. Somehow, she tripped and ended up falling and badly spraining her ankle. But despite the pain, she told us that she couldn't go to the doctor because at the time, five little girls and the one she was carrying were desperately depending on her. So what did she do? She bandaged her ankle up with some old rags made from one of her house dresses and continued to hang the clothes on the line—her babies needed those diapers, clean and dry. What a marvelous example of strength, tenacity, and endurance, and most importantly, *love!*

I will forever be indebted to my incredible mother for being a strong and beautiful woman, who, in spite of immeasurable odds, managed to raise seven girls, whom I have aptly named "Ora's Girls."

I thought it would be great to record in writing, and share the simple yet profoundly important "motherly" anecdotes that my mother shared with my sisters and me while growing up. These anecdotes, along with a plethora of life lessons, helped shape us into the women we are today.

Wisdom from years past isn't readily offered to our youth today. It seems to me that this country is rapidly becoming a society of selfishness and one completely unaware of the importance of imparting meaningful lessons. It's imperative that we share the lessons we learned from our elders in order to help people live a more fulfilling and selfless life.

My greatest hope is that as you peruse the many lessons my mother taught me, along with the many life-changing stories that occurred as a result of the lessons, that it will evoke beautiful and meaningful memories from your past while igniting a desire deep within to seek out meaningful and lasting relationships with loved ones and strangers alike. I share these stories not as guide for you to follow, but rather as a window through which you may see the life I lived and know how I came to be the woman I am today.

Lastly, I ask that you purposely seek out unbiased wisdom to help you learn and navigate this circuitous journey—LIFE.

I humbly and proudly dedicate this memoir to my beautiful mother, Ora.

I will always love you.

-Momma-
"A woman gives birth, but a mother gives life." Carla J

*"First impressions are
lasting impressions."*

"First impressions are lasting impressions."

You really only get one opportunity to make a first impression. There are really no do-overs with that. Slow down and think before you do something that you will regret for the rest of your life. Sometimes the words that come out of your mouth don't always check with your brain first. If you have time to prepare before sharing your opinion, practice STPA: Stop, Think, Plan, and Act. It's probably a good idea to keep this thought in mind with everything you do.

A lot of people will judge you simply based on the way you dress, speak, or even smell. If you are about to make a first impression and you are unsure if you are dressed to impress or unsure of how to act or what to say, and you genuinely care, ask a family member or close friend for their honest opinion. Then please be open and receptive when they give it to you, too.

While growing up, my mother made sure that all six of my sisters and I looked our very best before we left the house. We didn't have much, but we took good care of the little we had. She also told us that we had better always be on our best behavior, too, because the world was always watching when we least expected.

Well, the world is always watching, and you just might want to make sure that the first impression that anyone receives about you is actually the person you want them to meet. Caring what others think about you should not be laborious, but it should be on your radar.

"Get up early if you really want to have a productive day."

"Get up early if you really want to have a productive day."

Unless you are working the graveyard shift, frequently sleeping late may cause you to miss out on life and all of the great things it has to offer. Get up! Gather your thoughts and plan for a productive day. There are so many things that you can do in the morning to help you have a better day: plan, pray, meditate, read, apply for a job, get to work early, clean, cook, exercise, or simply sit in a quiet place and listen to birds singing as you plan your day. As crazy as this may sound, I really feel that somehow God is closer to His children in the still of the mornings. If you've ever noticed, birds sing the loudest in the morning. I believe they are probably communicating with God.

It may be hard to do at first, or it may even feel initially as if things aren't much different, but stay the course and positive results are bound to follow. My mother worked as a maid when it was called "day's work." She also drove a school bus for fifteen years. Both jobs required her to get up in the wee hours of the morning to start her day. On numerous occasions, I can vividly remember waking up for school only to find a pan of freshly baked homemade biscuits baking in the oven, multiple loads of clothes washed, dinner prepared for later that day, and an immaculately clean house. My mother had done all of this before the break of dawn and before she would go to work.

On Saturday mornings, there was no such thing as "sleeping late" or "sleeping in." All six of my siblings and I knew the routine all too well. Saturday mornings were meant for cleaning and preparing for the next week. As frustrating as it was for me at that time, I did it and never talked back—at least not loud enough for her to hear.

I would also often see my mother on her knees praying early in the morning. She would always say that she wanted to thank God first thing in the morning for all of the things He was going to do for her that day.

For me, getting up early was and continues to be a blessing in my life. I hope it's a blessing for you, too.

"If you can't say anything nice, don't say anything at all."

"If you can't say anything nice, don't say anything at all."

Some people feel that they always have to say something or give input when others talk about something. But listening is far more valuable than speaking. It greatly aids you with knowing when to speak and what to say when it's time.

You probably know someone who literally makes you cringe when you see them coming your way, simply because they are always saying something negative about something or someone. If you happen to be that "someone" who talks too much, learn to look for cues from loved ones, friends, and colleagues, so that you will know when to respond and when to listen. Your friends may not always tell you when you've said something you shouldn't, but you can tell just by the look on their face. So, learn to listen. Be a good steward over the words that come out of your mouth. One thing is for sure—once you give sound to your thoughts, it's too late. You can never get those words back.

My mother once told me about a time when she and a good friend of hers were sitting in church one Sunday morning and she noticed a lady walking into church wearing a strange-looking fur piece. My mother said she leaned over and asked her friend, "Girl, what is that she's wearing? It looks like farm fur or something, and she's wearing it as if it is a pure sable mink." My mother said that as she continued to talk, she noticed her friend was really quiet and looking at her in a strange way. She immediately asked her, "Girl, what's wrong with you?"

Her friend slowly leaned towards her and said, "Uh, well, I gave her that fur for her birthday. I thought it was a nice gift."

Needless to say, my mother learned a very important lesson that Sunday morning! "If you can't say anything nice, don't say anything at all, because sometimes 'silence' can be your best friend."

"Don't tell your business,
if you don't want it repeated."

"Don't tell your business, if you don't want it repeated."

You and God are the only ones who are guaranteed to keep your secrets. No matter how close you think you are to someone, the likelihood of them keeping your innermost thoughts and secrets that you share with them are slim. Asking God for discernment when it comes to choosing people to confide in will prove useful. Learning to deal with serious issues on your own will also serve you well, too.

There's not much worse than confiding in someone who you think will keep your innermost secrets, only to find out that they have shared them without your permission. That's sad yet sometimes inevitable. The only way to prevent something like this from occurring is simple: *Don't tell what you don't want repeated.* Now I do know that not "everybody" you tell your business to will tell it to others, but it's simply not uncommon for people to tell your secrets. For some people, gossiping and sharing other folk's business is an addiction.

One thing is for sure, when someone else tells your business, it will never again be told exactly the way you initially told it. "Your business" will definitely take on a life of its own.

I am so glad my mother was not a gossiper. While highly opinionated, she never gossiped. "Even beautiful people look ugly when they gossip," she'd say. I don't ever recall hearing my mother on the phone or sitting amongst friends telling her business or the business of her loved ones. She led by example and all seven of her girls followed suit.

So remember, if you do choose to tell someone your business, be selective when choosing a confidant. And keep in mind that the likelihood of them telling someone else is highly probable. My mother's oft-repeated reminder remains with me to this day. Whenever I think about sharing my secrets, I can hear her telling us now, "A dog who brings a bone will certainly carry one. Watch your friends, girls. Watch your friends."

"*A dog that brings a bone will certainly carry one.*"

"*A* dog that brings a bone will certainly carry one."

If someone comes to you and tells you private or disrespectful things about other people, you can certainly believe that they are telling private and disrespectful things about you to others, too. Gossiping looks ugly on everybody. My mother used to tell me, "Don't deliver garbage. Don't receive it, either." In other words, don't always be the one who people can count on for hearing messy and negative news.

Also, don't be the one who people can always drop their "garbage" on, as well. As interesting as gossip often is, don't let gossiping folks think that you are the one they can unload it on. Hearing these stories can disrupt your performance on the job and even affect you physically and mentally. Carrying someone else's gossiping garbage can be laborious and complicated.

Moreover, gossiping is a dangerous tool that many people use to tear others down while trying to prevent anyone from actually seeing *their own deficiencies*. Some people are so dissatisfied with themselves, but because they lack the courage or the wherewithal to change, they go through life being miserable while constantly trying to make others feel miserable too. One way they do this is by spreading vicious lies about the people who are closest to them.

Thus, gossiping is also a form of bullying. It can destroy long-standing relationships and even be the reason behind tragedies such as acquiring an eating disorder, committing suicide, or even possessing a lifelong feeling of self-hate.

So be careful not to make it a habit of talking about others when they are not around or even being a part of conversations that involves talking badly about someone who's not present. It's really simple—gossiping is an ugly trait. And it's just plain mean!

"Don't always wear your feelings on your sleeves."

"Don't always wear your feelings on your sleeves."

Some folks go through life so vulnerable that when a slight wind laced with trouble blows their way, it throws them completely off of their feet. Their family and friends tip-toe around them, afraid that they will say something or do something that offends them. If that's you, let me just say, *toughen up!* Life throws everyone curve balls. If the world knows that you're that fragile, you will get every ball known to man thrown at you all at once, while the jokesters hide the catcher's gloves and watch the lumps rise on your head!

Early in life, I learned that the world could be a cruel place to inhabit and that if I wanted to get anywhere, I wouldn't get there by being an emotional wreck. My son depended on me to be his rock and I was determined not to let him down. Having him look up to me spurred me on to being a strong woman—the strong mom that he desperately needed and loved.

My mother was a tough woman who refused to fall apart, especially in front of her girls. If any of the girls started crying after getting into an argument or fight, my mother would storm into the room and say something like, "Okay, that's enough of that crying! Suck it up! If you're crying like that over this, the world will make you weep over far more than that." She didn't want her girls to be weaklings. She knew that the world could really be a tough place and that only the strong ones truly survived. The others just existed.

"*Some people will use you
if you let them.*"

"Some people will use you if you let them."

There will always be someone, somewhere, who will use you if you let them. Keep yourself guarded. Don't overlook the obvious. Sit down and make a list of the pros and cons of questionable people in your life. If the cons outweigh the pros, check them or drop them. Continuing to be friends with people who don't have your best interest in mind will inevitably start to feel like a weight or yoke around your neck. *Shake them off!*

Some people spend a lifetime trying—and often succeeding—to use other people to their advantage. Oftentimes, it's simply just a matter of standing up to the person who's trying to use you. After you've carefully surveyed a situation and it becomes clear that someone is trying to use you, let them know in no uncertain terms that you do not plan on being a human doormat.

My mother taught all of her girls that people have a tendency to treat you the way you act. Sometimes we have to teach people how to treat us. That may sound weird, but it's actually true. For example, my mother taught all of her girls, "If you act like a nut, you'll be treated like a nut!" If you find yourself constantly being treated with disrespect, stop and take stock of the vibes you're giving off. You might be surprised to discover that "like attracts like."

On the other hand, you don't have to always be an "eye spy." Relax and enjoy life. Stop hiding in the bushes to try to see what someone is really doing when you're not looking. Stop checking other folk's cell phones, Facebook, Snapchat, and Twitter accounts.

While growing up with seven girls in the house at one time, there was always something going on. Somebody was always getting into something.

If something was broken or not where it was supposed to be, my mother would line us up in a row and ask us one by one, "Ok, who did it?" If no one came forward, she would often say, "That's all right. It'll come out! Eventually, *it will all come out!*" As sure as the sun rose and set, whatever one or more of us had done, it would eventually come out.

Don't waste an abundant amount of time trying to figure out the ulterior motives of others or what's really going on in a particular situation. Just be yourself, do the right thing, stand back and watch things unfold, because *they will unfold*.

Life is really much too short to spend time trying to track the causes and actions of someone else's behavior. As my mother used to say, "What goes in the wash, will definitely come out in the rinse." Hopefully you won't be the one who supplied the dirt.

"*Don't always look for validation from others.*"

"*D*on't always look for validation from others."

No one else should really know you better than you know yourself. Stop *always* going around looking for validation from those who aren't really qualified to give it to you. When you get up to start your day, stop and take a good look at yourself in the mirror and say, "*Today,* I will be the best person that I can be. I love me. I am not what I should be, but I'm working towards being a better person every day. I'm a constant work in progress, and today I choose happiness and a good life. I will not let snide remarks and side-eye looks steal my joy because I know who I am and can't no devil in hell stop that." If you adopt this attitude, inevitably self-validation will come. But first, it must come from you.

I once heard Oprah Winfrey say, "Everyone wants validation from someone at some point in their life." Some folks will dispute that, but honestly, I believe it. *All of us* want validation in some form or another at some point in our life. There's nothing necessarily wrong in that. Just don't lose yourself in what others think or don't think about you.

Once when I was a little girl, I came home from school crying because a classmate had called me ugly. My mother told me something that remains deeply embedded inside me. She said, "Honey, let me tell you something. First of all, you are a child of the King and that's something to celebrate every single day. He made you and He is pleased with all of His creations. Don't let some little loudmouth classmate steal your joy. Know your worth! You are an heir to the King who sits on His throne. Just own it!"

"Don't always look for something in return when you do a nice gesture for someone."

"Don't always look for something in return when you do a nice gesture for someone."

Sometimes nice gestures will be recognized and appreciated by others and sometimes they will not. This may occur either because people are too caught up in themselves to acknowledge you and what you've done or maybe no one bothered to teach them how to respond when someone does something nice for them. That makes it all the more important for you to do things for others simply because you choose to and not because you are looking for anything in return.

It's really unfortunate, but some people live their life with a sense of entitlement and think if others do anything nice for them, it's because they should have done so. It's quite simple: they think they deserved it. When you do something kind or meaningful for anyone, let your greatest reward come from within. People who always have one hand held out with the purpose of giving and the other hand held out with the expectation of receiving, have a convoluted idea about the true concept of giving.

My mother would often tell us when you find someone who acts generously and who doesn't expect anything in return—except a simple "thank you"—you're looking at a person who is truly connected with God and fully understands what giving is all about. Even the Bible tells us to give and not expect anything in return. Jesus reminds us to "love your enemies, do good to them, and lend to them without expecting to get anything back. Then your reward will be great, and you will be children of the Most High, because he is kind to the ungrateful and wicked." (Luke 6:35 NIV)

I am so glad my mother taught me that my true rewards for giving will never come on this side of heaven. I will continue to give because it's the right thing to do, and it pleases God.

"Never get too big
to apologize."

"Never get too big to apologize."

Too much pride is an unattractive attribute on anyone. It doesn't matter who you are or what profession you have, apologizing at some point is inevitable. Apologizing when you have mistreated someone is not only the right thing to do, but it sets an example for others to emulate. A person who thinks they are too important to apologize is a difficult person to be around and to love.

My mother used to always say, "If you did something wrong, own up to it, apologize, and move on." She wasn't one to mince words. She'd also admit that she'd made a lot of mistakes in her life and hurt some people along the way, but she was never too proud to apologize. If any of us girls would get into a fight with another sister, my mother would always make us immediately get together and apologize. Sometimes, I really had no clue what I was apologizing for, but when my mother told any of her to girls to do something, you didn't ask questions. You just did it.

There are certainly going to be times in your life when you may or may not have done something wrong to offend someone; however, if someone feels offended, simply apologizing and acknowledging their hurt can make a world of a difference. Don't let pride or anger prevent you from doing what's right. One thing is for sure: Tomorrow isn't promised. Refusing to give an apology owed to someone is simply too heavy of a burden to carry for a lifetime. Learn to release that stubborn pride and live a more fulfilling life. It's truly worth it.

"What goes around will definitely come back around sooner than you think."

"*What* goes around will definitely come back around sooner than you think."

Whether you believe in God or not, what you do to others and for others, whether it is good or bad, will definitely come back to you. It's simply called karma, and *karma* is real. My mother used to say that a great portion of a person's future was definitely a repeat of what they had done in their past, but with a greater effect. Although I didn't quite understand that idea while growing up, I've lived long enough to fully understand exactly what she was talking about. You do good things and good things will come back to you. You do bad things and bad things will come back to you. My mother referred to it as "reaping what you sow."

I now live my life with purpose and I always keep the idea of "harvesting" in the forefront of my mind. I only want to plant seeds of hope, seeds of love, and seeds of inspiration because I know that what I put out into the atmosphere is exactly what I am going to get in return. I purposely surround myself with people who believe this, too.

My sisters and I witnessed our mother living a life full of dignity and respect. She was an honest and upright woman who taught her girls that we could never go wrong by treating others well.

One of her favorite sayings when my sisters and I were growing up was, "You got to reap what you sow, child. You got to reap what you sow." She would say that when one of my siblings or I would do something unpleasant or disrespectful to another sister. She'd look us straight in the eyes as she said it, and we'd see the disappointment written there. None of us ever wanted to hear her say those words to us. We'd immediately apologize and promise to never make that mistake again.

"Common sense isn't always common!"

"Common sense isn't always common!"

Just because someone appears to be extremely intelligent doesn't mean that they have common sense, so don't just assume they do. With so many advancements in technology, people are rarely required to think things through anymore. "Click here," "click there,"—and *voilà!* Answers are provided without much brain work at all.

The easiness of life today makes it all the more imperative that older adults teach children and younger adults the value of thoroughly thinking things through before implementing decisions. Although common sense isn't always common, pausing and thoroughly thinking things through will undoubtedly prove to be helpful more times than not. My mother would often tell me, "Girl, figure it out!" She wasn't quick to hold our hand and walk us through everything. She wanted all of her daughters to be thinkers. She wanted us to grow up and be productive citizens—intelligent citizens who could do more than just cope, but thrive, in spite of good or bad circumstances. She knew that if she coddled us and didn't allow us to "fall and bump our heads" while trying to figure things out, we were doomed to failure. I can honestly say that those were some powerful lessons; however, I am sincerely thankful for "the bumps" because they are directly responsible for making me the woman I am today. Having common sense can truly be innate for some and a complete mystery for others.

Although my mother never obtained a high school diploma or attended college, she was a very smart woman. Oftentimes, she had to trust her instincts when it came to making tough decisions. If my siblings or I would struggle, trying to figure out the solution to a problem, my mother wasn't quick to come to our rescue. She allowed us to work things out on our own because she knew that it was the difficult experiences that built character and character built lives.

"Do not be a borrower."

"Do not be a borrower."

People tend to avoid someone who's always looking or asking for something. No matter how often your family or friends say that borrowing from them is "not a big deal," *it really is a big deal!* Learn to earn your own way. Save your money or do something legal to earn more. My mother used to say, "Baby, it's not *if* a storm or rainy day is coming, it's **when** it's coming. So be prepared!"

I know all of us at one point or another will need help with something and may even have to borrow money. That's life! Just make sure that you are not always the one who's in need. Be a good steward over your finances—not someone who's always watching everyone else's wallet or purse when it opens.

Nothing is more disturbing than seeing someone who's always borrowing your money, yet spending their own money frivolously. Even the Bible makes many references to folks who borrow. For example, in Psalms 37:21 it says, "The wicked borrow and do not repay, but the righteous give generously," and "The rich rule over the poor, and the borrower is slave to the lender" (Proverbs 22:7).

My mother always kept a stash of cash around the house for what she termed as "a rainy day pot." With seven daughters, inevitably there were many "rainy days." She would hide it anywhere she thought a burglar wouldn't look if they broke into our home. She occasionally hid money in a sugar container, cookie jar, shoes, socks, or even a coffee can in the refrigerator. Now that's what you call "cold cash."

"*Don't try to be big when little got you.*"

"Don't try to be big when little got you."

This quote was one of my mom's most favorite sayings. Not much else disturbed her more than folks trying to pretend to be more important than what they really were or pretending to have more than what they really had, simply to impress others. My mom would often say, "Stevie Wonder can even see that they are faking it!"

With social media being the craze, it appears as if a lot of people are pretending to be happier, richer, and even skinnier than they really are. My mother used to also say, "Everything that glitters ain't gold, y'all."

Trying to be something you are not is a tedious and back-breaking job. Why spend your life laboring to be someone you are not? Embrace who you are and what you have. If you're not happy with it, change it. Of course, change isn't always easy and it definitely won't come overnight, but at least you will feel better about yourself. That wool you think you are pulling over other folk's eyes can be used to make socks or a cuddly scarf instead.

As a child, I can remember always wanting to have more than what we had—better clothes, better shoes, a better home, and the list goes on and on. But Mom gave us the best she had to offer and when she sensed that we were being ungrateful, she would quickly remind us that God wasn't overly concerned about us acquiring things, but that He was more concerned about the love we had in our hearts for each other. So, please live your life instead of trying to live someone else's fairytale lifestyle. It makes for a more fulfilling life.

"Give a person a fish, they will eat for a day, but teach them how to fish, they will eat for a lifetime."

"Give a person a fish, they will eat for a day, but teach them how to fish, they will eat for a lifetime."

Self-preservation is a great ability to possess. Learning how to take care of yourself in any situation is a priceless lesson to learn. Handouts should really be "hand-ups." My mother taught all seven of her girls how to be responsible and to survive with little or nothing. Essentially, she taught her girls "how to fish." She wasn't great at giving out handouts without them being accompanied by some bit of practical advice.

Prior to my mother meeting my stepfather and giving birth to my youngest sister, she raised six girls on her own. My mother worked multiple jobs to ensure that we had the bare necessities of life. She didn't ask for or expect handouts. She worked hard and learned to make do with what she had.

One particular year, I can vividly remember being thrilled about my school's upcoming May Day dance. This was a huge event held every year in May. All of the girls were asked to wear adorable white dresses and perform these beautifully orchestrated dances on the playground. This particular year had been exceptionally tough on my family and I. I remember going to my mom to let her know that I needed a white dress for the upcoming dance. She immediately told me that she just couldn't afford it this year. My heart dropped. The thought of not getting a white dress for the "May Day" dance crushed me. I could tell my mother sensed my sadness because later that day she came to me and told me that she was indeed going to get me a beautiful white dress for the dance. When I asked her how, she just replied, "God made a way." At the time, I didn't quite understand how "God made ways," I was just glad He made them.

I later discovered that my mother had torn up an old bed sheet and had hand sewn me a dress that was simply lovely.

My beautiful mother did not let the fact that she couldn't afford anything for her girls prevent her from at least attempting to make us happy. But she gave me something far more precious than a dress that day. I will be forever indebted to her for teaching me the value of "learning how to fish" and surviving on what you have.

"Call a stone a stone."

"Call a stone a stone."

Don't always be indecisive because you lack courage. When you have to give your opinion, remember to practice STPA: Stop, Think, Plan, and Act! Stop wavering like a ship without a sail. People will quickly lose respect for you and will definitely not take you seriously. If it stinks, *it stinks!* If it's good, fair, or right, *say it* and move on! Just keep in mind, your goal should not be to offend or deliberately hurt someone's feelings, but rather to speak in an honest, fair, and loving way. You want to always try to be the one that when someone is in need of advice, they can come to you because they know that you are going to be honest and upfront with them. That type of friendship is priceless.

Double-talking is unattractive, no matter who's doing it. Saying one thing while meaning something else is an unattractive trait on anyone. Some politicians are known for telling voters one thing prior to an election, then delivering totally the opposite of what they promised once they win. Frustrating, right? So don't you do it, either.

My mother would often say, "Stop talking out of both sides of your mouth at the same time! For goodness's sake, say what you mean, and mean what you say!" That advice has served me well and continues to do so to this very day.

For the longest time, I struggled with being upfront with people for fear of hurting their feelings, only to realize that I wasn't being a true friend if I wasn't going to be upfront with them. Again, it's important to "call a stone a stone," as long as you do it with honesty, respect, and love.

"*Poop or get off the pot.*"

"Poop or get off the pot."

Sometimes you just have to make a decision and go for it. Continuing to be indecisive about an issue, or even being indecisive about whether or not someone should be in your life, can get really old really fast. Your family and friends only care to listen to your same old sad song for so long. They will even throw you a pity party with your favorite cake and colored balloons, but if you keep talking about dealing with the same thing over and over and never doing anything about it, they are apt to run every time they see you coming. They will also clap when they see you going and definitely stop taking your tired phone calls, too. Nagging even gets old to a dog. Deal with the issue and move on.

My mother had to make a lot of decisions—tough decisions—and sometimes she had to make them in a moment's notice. Rarely was she given the luxury of having more than enough time to make decisions.

Once when I was really young, my mother could no longer afford the large apartment that we lived in at the time, so she gathered all of my sisters and me in the living room and told us that we would be moving to a much smaller apartment and there was absolutely nothing we could do about it. My youngest sister started to cry. My mother picked her and told, her, "I am responsible for all of y'all and although this is tough on me, too, it's just something that has to be done." She kissed her on the forehead and told her, "Now get upstairs and start packing your stuff."

My mother was a very wise woman. At times, I was overwhelmingly amazed at how decisive she was during some of the toughest times of her life. Looking back, I now know that she was probably afraid and at times she probably didn't know exactly what to do, but because she had seven little girls depending on her, she simply did what she had to do and she did it well, too.

*"A closed mouth
doesn't get fed."*

"*A* closed mouth doesn't get fed."

Speak up, especially when you really need to. People will start using you as a human doormat if you don't speak up for yourself. No matter how you may think someone else possesses the ability to read your mind, they really can't. Learn to respectfully make your request known and speak up when the time is right. There are thousands and thousands of folks standing in line to lay on doctors' sofas, ready to pour out their hearts simply because they have allowed themselves to become a human doormat in life. Ask for discernment and strength from God to know when and how to speak up for yourself. After all, there are a lot of folks walking around looking skinny and gaunt because they suffer from "closed mouth" syndrome. That's never a good look.

I had my son when I was young. I learned early in life as his mother that I had to speak up for the both of us if I was going to get what we needed. I didn't always know exactly what to say or exactly how to say it, I just knew *I had to say it!* He was my son and it was my responsibility to raise him to be a productive and kindhearted young man. I was the one who had to make sure that he had the best life I could give him. Advocating for him and myself made that possible.

My mother would often say, "Speak up, child. Ain't nobody a mind reader. The world will use you up real quick if you don't speak up!" I firmly took those words to heart and I am mighty glad I did.

*"Anybody can teach
you something."*

"*A*nybody can teach you something."

It doesn't matter who you are in life or where you are from, you still possess the ability to teach anyone a life lesson. Life lessons don't discriminate and they come in multiple forms through many people and experiences. My mother would often tell my sisters and I that when folks get too old, too rich, or too smart to receive sound advice, it was definitely time for them to check into "Cemetery Motel" or "Golden Gate Inn" because only the grave was the proper place for people who thought that way.

Some of life's most important lessons come when you least expect them. Don't shun anyone because you think they don't have something worthy of being said. Life's lessons don't always come immediately or in the way you think they will come. Expect the unexpected in the most unexpected ways.

My mother used to say, "A bum in a ditch can teach you something." She treated everybody with respect because she thought everybody was important and worthy of being treated well. It didn't matter if he was the milkman or a clerk in a store, she treated everyone all the same—with respect. She knew it was the right thing to do and I never saw her waver.

Although my mother only had an eighth grade education, she remained open to the idea that "anybody can teach you something" until the day she died. Because of that, she lived a blessed and fulfilled life. She was smart enough to receive sound advice, no matter the messenger, and thankfully she taught all seven of her daughters to do the same.

"Your beauty will only get you so far."

"Your beauty will only get you so far."

You have to connect your outside beauty with your inside beauty for it to truly work. If you are only beautiful on the outside, people will realize it soon. While they might treat you well in your presence, they'll turn to criticize you behind your back. Periodically, stop and take a deep introspective look within to make sure that your inside beauty matches your outside beauty. After all, a double dose of beauty is far more beneficial.

I have been around a lot of people who believed that because they were beautiful, they had the right to treat others as if they didn't matter simply because of the way they looked or didn't look. I have also been around people who believed that "beautiful people" had sort of an ordained right to treat others differently. After all, they were beautiful, right? Wrong! No one has the right to treat anyone disrespectful because of the way they look, talk, walk, or choose to live their life.

My mother taught her girls to make sure that our hearts were far more beautiful than what was visible on the outside. She would often say, "Girl, you need brains to make it in this cold world. Your beauty will fade, but the love shared from your heart will last forever." My mother was a beautiful woman, but she never used her beauty to gain an advantage over anyone or anything. Her heart was pure and she never treated anyone differently because she herself had been given a "double dose of beauty."

"Don't be a loose goose!"

"Don't be a loose goose!"

Being loose with your body is one of the quickest ways for a woman or a man to lose respect from others. My mother had seven girls and she constantly warned us about not being "loose with our bodies." When we were growing up, promiscuity was not common and was greatly frowned upon.

Unfortunately, I had to learn this very important lesson the hard way. When I was just sixteen years old, I met my son's father and fell in love. Because of a lack of knowing my self-worth, I didn't heed my mother's advice and lost myself in his brokenness. Months later, I became pregnant. I was ashamed and hurt. The last thing I wanted to do was to hurt my mother. She'd had a rough life and me getting pregnant at sixteen only made things that much more difficult for her.

Today, promiscuity seems almost like the status quo. Big media personalities are telling us that it is okay to "test the waters" before "dipping into or drinking it."

My mother never sat my siblings and I down to have the "birds and the bees" talk. She said her mama didn't have it with her and she wasn't about to have it with us. I really believe she was just uncomfortable talking about things relating to sex with her girls. What she did do was to tell all my siblings and me, "Girls, let me tell you this, these boys out here want one thing and one thing only, what you have between your legs. Don't let them smooth-talk you. You better be strong and keep your panties up and your dress down." Those were strong words for seven little girls, too. Although I love my son dearly and have no regrets that I am blessed to be his mom, at times I can't help but wonder, what would my life be like if I would have heeded my mother's advice.

"Your word ought to
be your bond."

"Your word ought to be your bond."

When you tell someone that you are going to do something, it's imperative that you do it. People usually take others at face value—until they can't. It is most annoying when someone tells you that they are going to do something and then they never do it. Don't be the type of person who rattles off empty promises just to please others. There's going to come a time, and far sooner than you think, when your word will be of the utmost importance. Don't find yourself in a predicament where no one believes what you are saying. You'll ask for help, but then it'll be too late.

When I was raising my only child at the time, I taught him to keep his credit in good standing and more importantly, to keep his "word" in better standing. I told him that people get flaws in their credit due to unforeseeable things happening like getting ill or losing their job. Nevertheless, if he would be an upstanding man who kept his word, he would always be blessed and a blessing to others.

If my mother said she was going to do something, whether it was cook your favorite meal or "whup your butt," that's exactly what she did. She was a woman who kept her word, no matter the cost. Being raised by a mother with integrity was one of the greatest gifts my mother could have ever given to herself and her girls.

And so I urge you: Purposefully choose to live a life of integrity. The rewards will be too numerous to count.

*"Always inspect
what you expect."*

"*Always* inspect what you expect."

Don't take for granted that just because you ask someone to do something and tell them how to do it, that they will do it to your satisfaction or even do it at all. You have to get in the habit of "inspecting what you expect."

If you expect honesty, inspect for it. If you expect loyalty, inspect for it. If you expect anything, learn to inspect it. Usually people will do a far better job when they know what they are doing is going to be inspected during and after completion. Set a standard of excellence by letting everyone around you know that you have high expectations and that you will inspect what you expect in a professional and non-offensive manner to ensure that your expectations are fulfilled. This includes family and friends, too. Inspecting what you expect will either get you deemed a nuisance or earn you major respect from others.

My mother always inspected what she expected from all seven of her girls. No matter if it was something as simple as cleaning our rooms or running errands outside of the house. Sometimes we even thought our mother had some type of "special powers" or something, because if we did anything we weren't supposed to do, somehow she would always find out. She was definitely a master at inspecting what she expected.

Inspecting what you expect doesn't always mean that you don't trust someone to do a job right. It sets the tone that you are someone who takes pride in what you do for others and you want others to take pride in what they do for you. Be leery of people who have a problem with you respectfully inspecting what you expect. If you are doing what you are supposed to be doing, you should not have a problem with anyone ever taking a closer look.

"You can't be a leader if you don't know how to follow."

"You can't be a leader if you don't know how to follow."

Sometimes it's just good to sit back and enjoy the ride. We don't always have to navigate the journey. A good leader knows when and how to follow. Great lessons can come when you take complete advantage of an opportunity to follow before being given the opportunity to lead. Learn to seize moments and observe all that surrounds you in every situation. You can learn from the good, the bad, and the ugly.

People who *always* want to lead instead of just being a part of the team will eventually find themselves alone. Poet John Donne once said, "No man is an island." I believe the best way to learn to be a leader is to learn how to follow. I have learned some powerful lessons simply just by being a great team member. As a follower, you have the freedom to observe the leader and learn from her successes and her failures. Eventually, when I did get the opportunity to lead, that priceless experience of being a team member served me well.

My mother never wanted to be a leader outside of the home. She often said that she was happy just being a team player. She may not have wanted to be a leader outside of the home, but she was the best leader at home. She taught all of her girls the importance of following instructions, being a team player, and that if we ever were given the opportunity to lead, that it was imperative to do it with integrity.

"Always work as if someone is watching."

"Always work as if someone is watching."

Don't slouch on the job or at any of your tasks just because you don't think anyone is watching. My mother used to tell all seven of her girls, "Someone is always watching you." How well you perform or complete a task should matter to you the most. I have received some of my biggest compliments and promotions simply by doing the best I could at whatever I was doing. Even when I didn't like what I was doing, I always did my very best and fortunately this attitude has always served me well.

Some people have missed out on great opportunities simply because they didn't take the job that they were assigned seriously, especially when they thought no one was watching. Sure, we all have bad days; however, those days should be few in numbers.

While growing up, I watched my mother get up early for fifteen years to drive a school bus to transport other peoples' children to and from school. My mother took pride in her job. She was never late and only missed work when she was ill. My mother taught all of her girls by example to "always work as if someone was watching." You never know what fledgling co-worker is watching you for guidance and leadership qualities or when a supervisor is watching for the next employee to promote. Hard work does eventually pay off. Always take pride in what you are doing or just don't do it at all!

I take great pride in everything that I do because I am a firm believer that others are always watching, and I truly want to be a positive example for all who are watching.

"I'm going to lay this at your feet, so you can either kick it or you can pick it up and use it."

"I'm going to lay this at your feet, so you can either kick it or you can pick it up and use it."

Some people do not like it when others tell them what to do or give them any type of sound advice, even if it's in their best interest. Then you have those who will always need advice watered down prior to giving it to them because they have a hard time accepting it.

My mother did not mince words. She said what she meant and she meant what she said. She'd say, "I'm going to lay this at your feet, so you can either kick it or you can pick it up and use it." I still find myself using this quotation to this very day, especially when I come in contact with someone I know who has a hard time receiving constructive criticism. It also appears that when I start off my advice with this quotation, somehow it's better received—probably because the advice comes with the option of accepting it or rejecting it.

I remember a particular time when this information served me quite well. I was having "relationship issues" with my son's father. I felt like I was going to have a nervous breakdown at any minute. I was not open to any kind of "I told you so" type of criticism from anyone, my mother included. Sensing that something was wrong, my mother came to me and said something that I will always remember, "Baby, I can tell you're going through something, so I'm going to lay this at your feet. You can either kick it or you can pick it up and use it. Life is entirely too short to live it unhappily and it is not that complicated, either—that is, if you don't make it complicated. You know exactly what you need to do to make whatever you are going through right. I want you to pray, ask God for direction, listen for Him to speak, trust His answer, and then move on to your happy place."

That was a profound word for my spirit that day. Looking back, that simple yet profound advice actually saved my life. I was at my wit's end and just didn't know what to do at the time. The situation had even begun to affect my parenting of my son.

I am so glad and grateful that my mother knew what wisdom to give me and how to give it to me at that particular time in my life. How you choose to communicate noteworthy advice to people can make a difference between them accepting your advice or discarding it. I am so grateful that I heeded my mother's advice that day. Now I can "lay it at your feet," too.

"*Treat others like you want them to treat you and yours.*"

"Treat others like you want them to treat you and yours."

Always treat people the way you want yourself and your loved ones to be treated. Learn to slow down and take an introspective look when you are about to interact with others to make sure that you are always treating them with respect. All of us want to be respected and treated fairly. We find it offensive and unnecessary when we aren't treated well by others. When you put yourself in the other person's shoes, you are more apt to do the right thing, no matter the situation.

Even if someone mistreats you, it's essential to remember that the right thing to do is to still treat them with respect. My mother used to say, "Two wrongs don't make a right." She was correct.

I know it may seem exhausting and frustrating to treat someone with respect when they have disrespected you, but don't let the way others treat you determine how you treat them. In life, there will always be people who just don't get the fact that they need to treat people respectfully. If you let their ignorance dictate your behavior, then it will be your character that gets diminished—not theirs.

My mother made sure that all of my sisters and I always treated others with respect. There were many times when we would go to our mother in tears because someone had mistreated us. My mother would often say that some people just don't know any better, and she'd urge us to remember to pray for them. She'd say, "You can't go wrong when you err on the side of right."

As I continue to live my life, I am often reminded that my mother was right. Time and time again, I've been blessed to be the recipient of many blessings, simply by choosing to treat people well and that is a rewarding feeling.

"Don't fight the inevitable."

"Don't fight the inevitable."

As a little girl, I can vividly remember hearing the song "Que Sera, Sera" while watching *The Doris Day Show*. I would run through the house for hours, singing and humming this song after every show. I loved the sound of it and I also loved what it meant, "Whatever will be, will be, the future is not ours to see..." Some things in life are inevitable. Your race, the family you were born into, and your physical abilities are some of the aspects of life that none of us have much control over.

When I was sixteen years old, I became pregnant with my son. It was one of the most difficult times of my life. I even attempted suicide. My son's father left me because at that time he wasn't ready to be a father. Being sixteen and pregnant at that time was not common. I felt like an outcast. Watching all of my friends living a life of a teen, while I had to give up so much to ensure that I was a good mom to my son, was unimaginably difficult. That was one of my lowest times ever. Nevertheless, I didn't fight the inevitable for long. I knew what needed to be done to ensure that my son had the best life that I could possibly give him. Though very difficult, I was committed to him and strived daily to ensure that he knew that he was the most important person in my life and that we were an unbreakable team.

My mother taught me by example to accept the things you can't change and change the things you can. She didn't sit around battling with many worries in her life. One of her favorite sayings was simple, yet profound: "If you can change it, change it! If you can't change it, move on before 'it moves over you!'" Needless to say, this idea has served me well.

109

"*Live your life and not someone else's.*"

"Live your life and not someone else's."

Stop comparing your life to someone else's life. Haven't you heard the old adage, "The grass always looks greener on the other side"? To that I say, "That is rarely the case. Learn to focus on your own grass!" If you are constantly trying to keep up with how your friends and the reality stars are living their life, you are headed for sure destruction. I am a firm believer that "not everything that glitters is gold."

True happiness will only come when you start living your life the way *you* want and need to live your life. It may look completely different from what others think you should be doing, but it's your life and only you can exist completely within you. Oftentimes we miss out on living the life we were meant to live because we are constantly trying to be someone else that we were not meant to be. Grasp your "true you." If you aren't happy with where you are in life or who you have become, stop and do an internal inventory. Then be courageous enough to get off the sidelines of life and make things happen.

My mother would often tell her girls, "We will not be a family that tries to keep up with the Joneses or the McCoys. We are who we are and that's it. We will not get caught up in trying to live someone else's fairytale." Wow, I can't even begin to tell you how those words helped me through so many rough patches while growing up. There were so many times when my sisters and I couldn't get the latest fashionable clothes or the super-cool hairstyles we had seen in the pages of *Jet* magazine, but we learned to appreciate what we had because we knew it was more important to spend time being ourselves. Our mother instilled in us the importance of not wasting a lot of time coveting someone else's blessings.

"*Take time to smell your flowers.*"

"Take time to smell your flowers."

Most of us spend entirely too much time building or maintaining a career only to acquire things that just aren't necessary. We become so involved that we fail to spend enough time enjoying the smaller things in life. Periodically, make time to have a good meal with your family and friends. Slow down and start appreciating the things that really bring you joy! Speak this to yourself frequently: Most of the "stuff" that you are moving so fast through life trying to acquire will outlast you. Live a life full of breathless moments. My mother used to say that there's one such moment that occurs every single day. You just have to slow down and look deep and hard enough to find it. It's the special moments that you'll want to recall in the end. Keeping a vase of your favorite fresh flowers in your home can serve as a constant reminder to take time to "smell the flowers" and live your life to the fullest.

My mother told all of her children long before her death, "I don't want a lot of flowers surrounding my casket at my funeral." When we asked her why, she said, "I am smelling my flowers now. I can't smell anything when I'm dead and gone."

I can truly say that my mother took advantage of multiple opportunities and enjoyed what she would often refer to as "her harvest" before she left this earth. I purposely and consistently find joy in the smaller things in life because I now know that those are the things that bring life's greatest rewards.

Some of my fondest memories are the times that I spend with my family. I am so grateful that my mother raised us to focus on the things that matter the most: faith and family.

"*Don't sleep on your destiny.*"

"Don't sleep on your destiny."

Some of us go through our entire life ignoring the plan that God has for us. Every man, woman, and child among us has a passion deep down that leads directly to their destiny. Sometimes we tell others what that is and for whatever reason, we don't work towards it ourselves. Then there are times when we don't tell *anyone* about our deepest desires. Sadly, there's more talent in the grave than on top of it. Most of us die with our "music having never been played" because we fail to adhere to that little voice deep within us that's telling us which path to take. What good is sheet music if it's never played for someone to hear? It is better to have tried and failed than to have never tried at all.

Please don't sleep on your destiny. There is no alarm clock to wake you. As the Bible encourages us, "work while it's day, because when night comes, no man can work" (John 9:4 NIV).

My mother would often say that "working while you have a clear mind and strength is far easier than working when you are disturbed and weak." Don't go through life procrastinating it away. Having regrets about something that you should have accomplished at a certain point in your life, can be very disheartening. My mother encouraged all of her girls to utilize the glorious rays of the sun while we could. What a beautiful and rewarding feeling it is!

"Do not ignore the
voice of life."

"Do not ignore the voice of life."

Some people go through life ignoring the plan or destiny that God has for their life because they refuse to listen to that little voice deep down inside of them.

I don't care who you are, you have that voice that speaks to you. Listen up, because it is trying to prevent you from making a big mistake, urging you to do the right thing, hinting for you to get what you need to get, pushing you to go where you need to go. Not heeding that voice at the right time in your life can lead to you making some of the worst decisions ever. It has gotten a lot of people into trouble, even costing them their lives.

Learn to tap into "you." Consider all the great leaders who chose not to ignore their inner voice and fortunately ended up rewriting history. Dr. Martin Luther King, Jr., Susan B. Anthony, Frederick Douglass, William Wilberforce, and Ida B. Wells—just to name a few. Each of these leaders fought against the floods of social opinions simply because they stayed tuned to that "still, small voice" inside of them. They did what they knew was right and the world is forever changed because of that choice. Although I am not "a great leader," I can say that when I've listened to my inner voice before making a tough decision, my life and my surroundings have always been the better for it. I can also say that many times I stubbornly didn't heed to my inner voice. As a result, I made huge mistakes; I've missed out on great opportunities, damaged relationships, and the list goes on and on.

Years ago, I experienced a difficult setback in my career. For a short period of time, I felt bitter and angry. But that little voice deep inside of me instructed me to do something different: *choose to become better and release bitterness.* I am so glad that I adhered to that voice because shortly thereafter, I was able to start a new and much more fulfilling career.

My mother encouraged all of her girls to listen for that "little voice." She told us it was God whispering His desires for our life into our hearts. She also said that we may not always like what that little voice was telling us; however, if we were obedient, the rewards would far outweigh the regrets. She was correct.

*"What will the footprints
of your life say?"*

"What will the footprints of your life say?"

When it's all been said and done, when you have given the last curtain call, when you have sung your last song and danced your last dance, what will the footprints of your life say about the life you've lived? I've heard some folks say that they don't care about what people will say about them when they are gone. Honestly, I really don't believe that. I really do believe that *everybody,* in some form or another, really does care about the legacy that they will leave behind when their life has ended.

We all have a responsibility to leave something noteworthy to those we leave behind. As we live our life, it should be one of substance and character. It should speak to those around us without having to utter a single word. I want my footprints to show love and respect for humanity.

Be leery of people who are always saying that they don't care what other people think about them. Now don't get me wrong—I don't believe that we should live our lives simply to please others. But what I do believe is that we should live a life full of examples that will bless people and inspire them to emulate.

My mother used to always say that she wanted to live a life that would speak for her long after she was gone. Everyone who knew my mother had nothing but nice things to say about her. She was a beautiful woman of grace and integrity, who genuinely cared about what the "footprints" of her life would say when she could make them no more.

Conclusion

Life truly has a way of teaching all of us unforgettable lessons. My mother was a beautiful and smart woman who had a passion for God, life, and family. I will always be grateful to her for the many lessons she taught my sisters and me. I am the woman I am today because of who she was and the thousands of lessons she taught all of her girls.

At my very lowest, my mother was there to lift me up. As I look back over my life, I know that I could not have made it without her. In spite of her displeasure with me getting pregnant at sixteen, she stood by me and helped me get through one of the toughest times in my life. As a teen mom, there were so many things that I didn't know in regards to raising a child. My mother didn't allow anything or anyone get in the way of being there for me.

She was also there for my sisters, too. All of us endured tough times for many reasons, but one thing remained constant: *our mother's unwavering love and support for her family.*

In 2008, my beautiful mother was diagnosed with Alzheimer's. She was seventy-eight years old. She died a year later. Even in the midst of struggling with this dreadful disease, in her own special way, my mother continued to express her undying love for her family. My family and I nurtured and cherished her until she took her last breath on this side of heaven. I will forever miss her and forever be indebted to her for the wisdom she left behind.

I am also happy to say that my biological father, Douglas, eventually stopped drinking and became an important part of his daughters' lives. Although he remarried, when asked years later what his greatest regret was, his response was quite clear, "I regret the day that I divorced your mother. I loved her then and I love her now."

Years later, my mother met and married my stepfather, Curtis. Together they had my youngest sister, Yolande. My stepfather loved our mother dearly. He would often say that his greatest gift was loving and caring for his queen: *my mother.* My stepfather died five months after my mother's passing. I really believe the cause of his death was a broken heart. He simply could not adjust to living a life without "his queen." They are together once again.

Sometimes life has really a strange way of teaching all of us many lessons. An important key to life is to pause occasionally and note the many life lessons being taught at every stage.

The late great Pastor Myles Monroe penned these unforgettable words in his book, *Understanding Your Potential*, "We are a sum total of what we have learned from all who have taught us, both great and small."

I emphatically know who I am because of the beautiful woman who raised me. My one petition to you is to choose daily to share something of substance with someone around you while cherishing sound advice from those who offer it. It's certain to make this place a better world to live in.

"Be someone's beautiful bright light in darkness."